# GEORGIA
## AND THE EDGE OF THE WORLD

# ROBIN BOYDEN

For my sister, Merryn.

Georgia and the Edge of the World
is A DAVID FICKLING BOOK

First published in Great Britain in 2021 by
David Fickling Books,
31 Beaumont Street,
Oxford, OX1 2NP

Text and illustrations © Robin Boyden, 2021

978-1-78845-179-6
1 3 5 7 9 10 8 6 4 2

David Fickling Books reg. no. 8340307

A CIP catalogue record for this book
is available from the British Library.

Printed by Grafostil, Slovenia.

Papers used by David Fickling Books are from
well-managed forests and other responsible sources.

'Georgia and the Edge of the World' first
appeared in The Phoenix, the weekly story comic.

www.thephoenixcomic.co.uk

Equine creature, take the girl.
This parchment will lead you to safety.

KABOOOOOM!!!

Look! There's a stumpy little creature headed this way.

I think it's a donkey.

Could be a pony?

It's a ponky!

Wait, it's carrying something. A baby?

Hah... a ponky.

Some years later...

HAPPY BIRTHDAY TO ME,
HAPPY BIRTHDAY TO ME,
HAPPY BIRTHDAY PRINCE GEORGE,
HAPPY BIRTHDAY TO ME!

18 years old, I'm finally a mature, respected adult...

And I got the wind-up horse I asked for!

Not even Georgia could ruin this day.

Huh?

TAP TAP

RAAAAAAH

RAAAH!

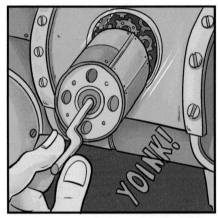

Look, Ponky, the Great Hall! Looks like a big celebration.

HAPPY BIRTHDAY GEORGE!

Inside...

Welcome, everybody. We have a grand unveiling soon, and pass the parcel.

But right now, say hello to the birthday boy...

...GEORGE!

It's me! You love me! Oh stop, too much!

Now, I promised I wouldn't make a speech, but I'm going to anyway.

Oh, great.

All I want to say is that my adopted sister, Georgia, is a disrespectful little oaf.

First she steals my horsey and then can't even turn up to my party.

I am absolutely furious with her.

26

29

You... you... child. You've ruined EVERYTHING!

You and that creature... I'll... I'll...

Now, George, I'll handle this. You calm down.

Georgia, why can't you be more mature, like your noble, heroic brother?

Adopted brother!

Get off my cake, you foul beast.

Prepare to meet thy maker, you cake taker!

Hero? He can't even lift his sword!

Sigh. When are you going to stop playing with all this junk and act like a proper lady?

I vowed to protect you, long ago, as my own child. So, for your own safety...

32

33

Stupid George, stupid Angleston.

Oh. Hi, Ponky. How are we going to get out of this one?

Why don't I fit in here? I can't go to etiquette school. That's not me.

These people don't understand me at all.

I don't want to be a lady, I want to be an adventurer!

Ponky! You brought my favourite book, The Lighthouse Keeper.

You always know how to cheer me up!

Listen to this, Ponky...

Ignatius and Isabella were engaged to be married.

But one day, an earthquake split the world, wrenching them apart.

Isabella built a lighthouse that would light the waves, searching for her lost love.

Ignatius, however, raged. He vowed to burn the world as his revenge.

The legend of Captain Ignatius Sidebottom was born, a man who swam with sharks.

Who climbed mountains, faced betrayal and capture. But no prison could hold him.

He won great battles aboard his ship, the Rotten Oyster, alongside his crew.

Meanwhile, Isabella continued her search for the man feared across the world...

The light showed her new worlds, people, nature, it adorned the stars.

But Ignatius eluded her. One stormy evening, the Rotten Oyster approached.

Isabella had to decide; shine the light and save Ignatius, or let Sidebottom perish.

Beyond his blazing beard of flames, Isabella saw the eyes of the boy she once knew.

Wouldn't it be great to find out what happened?

Not much chance of that stuck here though.

I need a miracle to get me out of Angleston.

Just one tiny miracle.

Oh, hello, what's this?

HELP

Later...

Nnngh. It's a bit tight!

Never fear, my gauntlet should have a handy tool for this...

Let's see. Magnifying glass? Nope.

Hairbrush? Useful, but not for this task.

45

It's not that simple. Myth is found at the end of the world.

The end of the world? I could be the greatest adventurer ever!

Wait... do you mean 'when the world ends' or 'the end of the world'?

At the edge of the Earth's surface is where you'll find Myth. A most magical place!

Well, my 'Earth is round' theory looks pretty stupid now.

I AM A GENIUS!

I know you're scared, Ponky...

48

But this is an opportunity – we need to go.

I'm going anyway, so if you want to keep me safe then you'll just have to come with me!

We could have an adventure like *The Lighthouse Keeper*.

Ew... ha ha

How would we ever get there though? We can't all fit in that bottle.

I have a few bits and pieces lying about the place.

All I need is an idea.

50

When George told me he saw you messing around this old relic, I had to intervene.

So you destroyed it?!

NOD NOD

My duty is to keep you safe. This building is not safe. Your silly inventions are not safe.

You will go to etiquette school or I shall have you locked up.

I'm already locked up!

NOD NOD

That's it. I'm leaving right now. Just need to find one thing first...

Sigh. Take her away.

Oh, there you are...

The Lighthouse Keeper

Freedom, sweet freedom...

Bright sunshine, shimmering sea and blue, blue sky...

...and those, what are those? Best check my books.

It will be hard to find an answer with this small selection.

According to my book, these sea creatures are called...

SHARKS...

...AND THEY EAT PEOPLE.

SAVE YOURSELVES!

RUN!

WE'RE DOOMED!

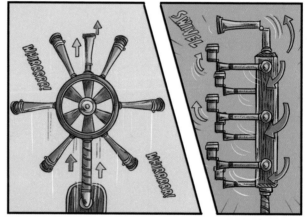

71

I think he wants you to copy him!

Hmm... I didn't have that in mind when I built the ship, but we can give it a go.

I know he looked after me, Ponky.

But I had to leave, didn't I?

There must be more to it. The Duke isn't a bad man...

...so why would he stop me following my dreams?

He blew up our workshop, Ponky!

And tried to make me wear a frilly dress! Gross.

It's just us now, Ponky.

And Lollylute of course.

You've helped us so much already, and we'll help you get your parcel to Myth...

...AND WE'LL ALL BE BEST FRIENDS!

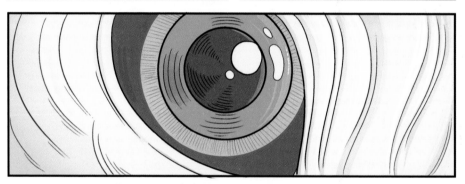

SQWAARKK...

Oh dear, it looks in some distress. Let's see if I brought anything with me that might help.

A saw? Maybe as a last resort, but too gruesome for my style.

Cake, the great healer. But that's mine. All mine.

Seems like the poor thing is a bit bloated.

Got any ideas how to fix this, Ponky?

SQWAARKK...

88

This one is my favourite.

Ah, *The Lighthouse Keeper*, an inspired choice. I know it well. Very well.

A grand tale of a lighthouse and a pirate ship...

YES! And the nefarious Captain Sidebottom, captain of the *Rotten Oyster*!

Terrorising the coast, doing wicked, wicked things!

Yes, but...

But one day, the *Rotten Oyster* is stranded in a storm, heading straight for the jagged rocks!

And the Lighthouse Keeper doesn't know whether to turn the light on and bring them to safety...

Yes, but...

...or to let them smash on the rocks and be rid of them once and for all!

IT'S AMAZING!

I SAID I KNOW IT WELL!

I apologise for shouting. I'm just excited to tell you this next part.

Every story is a myth. But by some unknown force of the universe they exist in the Land of Myth, where all our imaginations come to life.

I don't get it.

All it takes is a leap of faith, off the edge of the world.

And when you reach Myth, every hero, villain and monster you've ever read or heard of in a story can be found there.

So Lollylute's parcel... is for someone in a story I may have read?

It could be so. It's said that Myth is near when you reach the golden shores.

A coastline of washed up treasure, forgotten gems, silver swords and precious gold, lost at the edge of the world.

I COULD BE THE FIRST PERSON TO EVER EXPLORE MYTH!

That's the spirit! You are a true adventurer.

Our journey will be on land for the next part. Are you ready?

But what about *Patch*? We worked so hard on making him?

With all those books, you're clearly a bright young lady. You'll think of something.

Yeah! You're right. Thanks, Moo. I'll figure it out!

100

Later... The sails are made of silk from the extinct drunken spider...

...and it won the most awards at 'the boaties' last year.

GIRL.

Yep, you.

Spare an old man a drink?

The hot sun's got me cooked. Glad it's setting now.

A drink? Of course! Strawberry oat milk OK?

Aaah, much better.

Are you an adventurer too?

Aah, once I was. But I'm old and rusted out. This lot ain't got much use for me now.

But I like to think there's a little magic left in me.

105

Now let me do something for you.

Fairy creature...

...please may I borrow some of your sparks?

Put these on the flames.

Whoa! Ha.

FWOOOSSSHHHH!!!

FWOOOSSSHHHH!!!

Can you see the visions dancing?

Will I see the future? How exciting!

It's so bright, I can hardly see.

SPLASH

Don't put your faith in such silly illusions. Myth is the only place to see stories come to life.

Not here with this impostor.

Moo?

Now, we have an important package to deliver, don't we?

Let's go.

Why did you put the fire out? I wanted to see what was it was showing me.

The mind plays tricks, especially when you're in the dark.

You have to be more careful about who you trust.

You're right. I trusted the Duke and he tried to take everything from me.

Exactly.

Once we're past this valley, we'll be heading to the mountains.

I've never been to mountains! I'd better study for a while so I don't get caught out.

Excellent idea. Let's pause for a bit whilst you read your books.

Thanks, Moo, reading whilst we're moving makes me giddy.

SQWUAK

110

SQQQUAWWKK!

?

Stay quiet, the girl is just over there.

Now, take this...

...the location is marked on it. Don't be late.

Hey, Ponky. You look stressed. Are you OK?

Yes, Ponky, are you OK?

Good. Then let's get going.

We have valleys, mountains and forests to cross before we reach the edge of the world.

What a great view. We've travelled so far.

I think we should stop and rest here for the night.

I'm tired.

Yes, you do that. I'm going to catch some fish for breakfast.

Lollylute, come assist me.

I don't have to be bait do I?

YAWN!

All is going to plan, right on schedule.

It seems so.

Tomorrow we will reach the meeting place.

And then there shall be no escape.

I don't feel so good about this, Moo.

Well you have no choice, do you?

Have you forgotten what you are?

This time tomorrow, we will be on our way to Myth.

With the miracle girl locked in a cage at last.

Do we really have to put her in a cage? You put me in a bottle, it was very uncomfortable.

I did that out of spite. With Georgia, I can't take any risks.

But we're headed to Myth anyway, she wants to go!

Her ship won't survive the final part of the journey, the storms are too strong.

There's only one ship that could travel those seas, but I fear she won't board it willingly.

Moo! Give her a chance, she's already shown how capable she is.

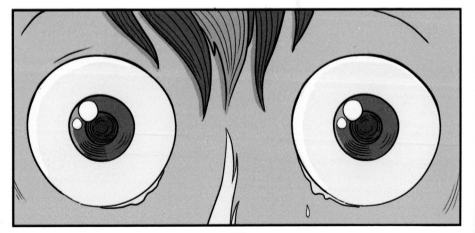

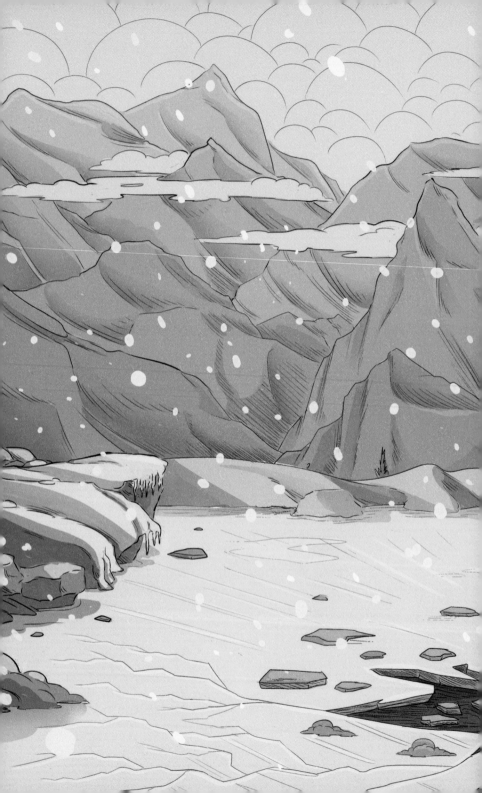

Don't you dare say anything to her.

We're close now. You can go back to who you were before all this mess began.

I'm not sure if I want to. Not like this.

It's not right.

Why didn't I jump in after him?

He could have been right there, freezing, crying for help.

I could have found a solution. That's what I've always done. Why not this time?

If you'd gone in the water, you would have suffered the same fate.

Don't say that. You were born to do this.

Ponky wanted to stop you at every turn.

He was a coward.

You're wrong! He protected me at every turn.

And I left when he needed me most.

I have to go back for him!

Georgia! There is no path back!

You can trust me.

But if you insist on leaving...

133

Luckily, I have a trick up my sleeve.

CLICK!

The Lighthouse Keeper searched the ship...

Just need a run up.

...but aside from some pelicans, there was no one around.

Almost there.

She couldn't help but feel that she'd walked into a trap.

SKID

WHAT ON EARTH?

135

138

Your dreams of heroics are bold and broad, but dreams can't compete with the blade of a sword.

You know how terrifying the pirates are... get in the pelican.

The *Rotten Oyster* from *The Lighthouse Keeper*? What's going on?

Welcome to your new home. I hear you're used to being trapped between walls.

No, no, please don't!

Show the child to her room.

AAAH!

FLLLOOOOOB

YOU!

Were you in on it from the beginning?

I had no choice. I belong to Moo.

I was sent to Angleston to draw you from the castle and bring you to her.

But why? What did I ever do to you, to any of you?!

You'll understand when we get to Myth.

I'm starting to think Myth isn't real. None of this was.

No. Myth is real. It's where you come from, Georgia.

No! I've never been outside of Angleston.

You're tricking me again, aren't you?

You lied about Myth. Why should I believe you?!

Because I was born in Myth too.

I don't understand.

Let me explain...

Moo created me.

Myths come alive when stories are written. And every story has a creator.

Including your favourite book...

...here ...look. This is the first edition.

The Lighthouse Keeper

by
Gloria Moon

What?

Once upon a time I lived in the lighthouse, searching day and night for those in distress.

At least, that's what Moo tells me.

I don't remember much, less each day. Just broken shards of an old dream.

And you trust Moo to fill in the blanks?

Of course not. But what choice do I have? I have no one, not even my memories, my self.

152

I was reborn as this: small and insignificant. Moo was all I had.

And she filled your head with stories too?

I woke up in the bottle you found me in. Moo was the first person I saw.

I was tasked to bring you to her.

The parcel was a trick, a lure. But one thing is true...

My parcel is for someone from Myth...

...and that person is you.

CLICK

WHIRRR

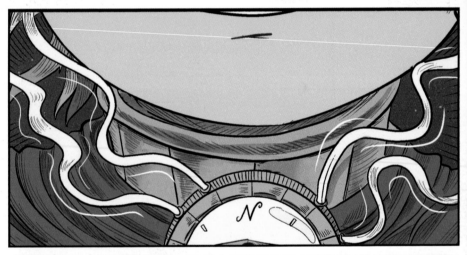

N

WHOOOSHHHH!!!

Better act quickly, before they catch up.

Now, where are you, Moo?

AHA!

164

You created me?

Georgia, get to a life raft!

Like, you're... my mother?

No, Georgia, I'm not your mother.

ZOOOM!

But I fear your father is trying to take this ship right now.

So MOVE IT!

Father?!

FWIIIII!

FWIIIII!

ZOOOM!

Moo?!

SHOVE!

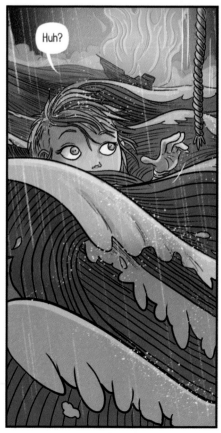

175

176

You rescued me?

Not my proudest moment, but unlike you I'm a good person.

Maybe one day you can forgive me.

I won't even consider it until you tell me what's going on.

As I mentioned, I created you, in the final chapter. And your father, he escaped Myth with you.

You mean the Duke? He's not my father and that wasn't an Angleston ship. I have seen it before, though.

No, Georgia, a real, or as close to a real father as you will have.

Why do you like my book so much, Georgia?

I'm not a great writer. It's not a great story. As far as I know, you're the only one that's read it.

Oh, I LOVE the characters! Ignatius and Isabella, they're great.

Of course you do. They're your parents.

The Lighthouse Keeper is my mother?

Captain Sidebottom is... MY FATHER?!

And you think he was the one who just sank the *Rotten Oyster*?

Yes, remember you said you saw that ship before.

Of course, the *Pilfering Pilchard*.

But what do they want with us?

I believe Sidebottom was recruiting a new crew.

He must have survived bringing you into this world...

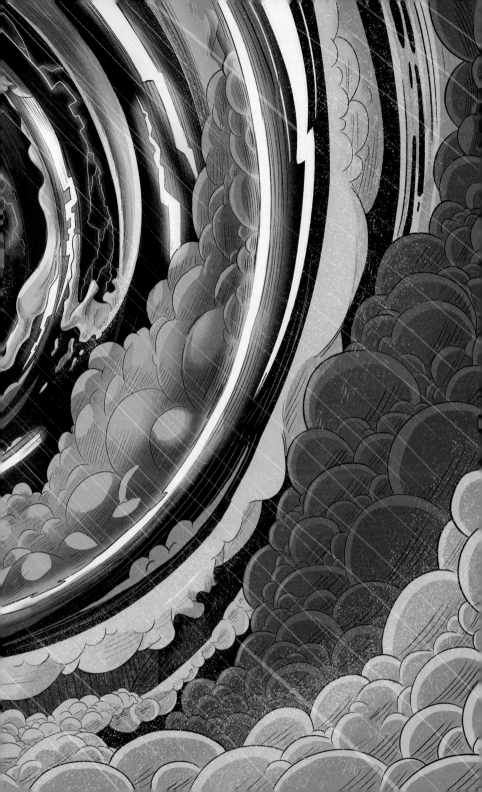

Gulp. Maybe we should turn back.

If you don't go on, you'll never know who you truly are. Even I can't tell you, you've been in this world too long.

Ponky, what do you think? I go where you go.

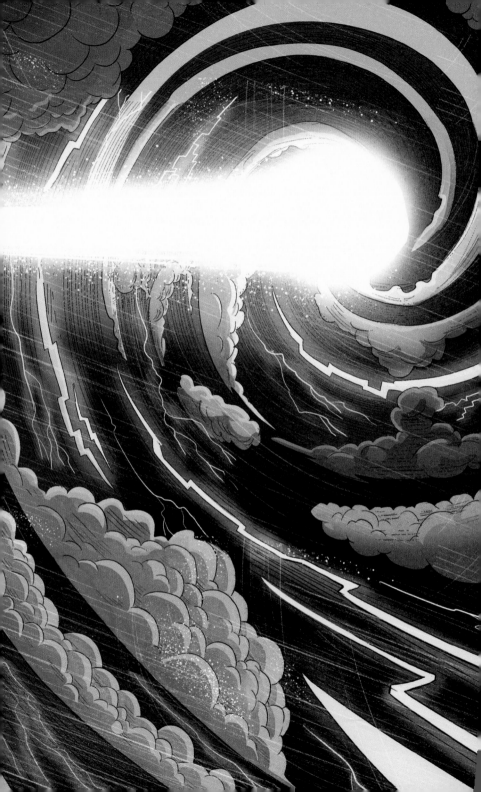

Whoa! Need to slow down now!

We made it through!

I felt her, I felt her warmth.

And it was emitting from you.

The compass belonged to the Lighthouse Keeper?

I think it belonged to your mother.

Together with my light...

...it showed us the way to go.

Hogwash.

There are horrors, monsters and villains there, far worse than me.

Darkness and sadness, bleaker than my own.

I lost my daughter, I lost everything, I lost Isabella...

...all because of her!

I'm sorry. I wasn't to know when I wrote it.

It was just a stupid story.

I'm NOT a story. I'm REAL!

Will all you adults just...be QUIET. For once.

I'm going to save my mum, wherever, whoever, she is.

Moo, if you're my creator and have power over me in Myth, can you give it up?

Well, I've never thought about it before. But I guess it's possible?

Well, then that's exactly what you're going to do. No more control, not over me, Lollylute, not any of us.

As you wish.

Good. Now all I need to do is follow the compass.

OK then... Let me just... hold on...

Are you sure this is pointing the right way?

I'm certain. We have to go...

This is it. This is why *The Lighthouse Keeper* isn't finished.

Because it's **MY** story.

What happens next is up to me.